Media Control

The Spectacular Achievements of Propaganda

SECOND EDITION

NOAM CHOMSKY

AN OPEN MEDIA BOOK

SEVEN STORIES PRESS / New York

ISBN: 1-58322-536-6 / ISBN-13: 978-1-58322-536-3

14   13   12   11   10   9

Cover design and photo by Greg Ruggiero.

Printed in Canada

CONTENTS

CONTENTS

MEDIA CONTROL

The Spectacular Achievements of Propaganda

THE ROLE OF THE MEDIA in contemporary politics forces us to ask what kind of a world and what kind of a society we want to live in, and in particular in what sense of democracy do we want this to be a democratic society? Let me begin by counter-posing two different conceptions of democracy. One conception of democracy has it that a democratic society is one in which the public has the means to participate in some meaningful way in the management of their own affairs and the means of information are open and free. If you look up democracy in the dictionary you'll get a definition something like that.

An alternative conception of democracy is that the public must be barred from managing of their own affairs and the means of information must be kept narrowly and rigidly controlled. That may sound like an odd conception of democracy, but it's important to understand that it is the prevailing conception. In fact, it has long been, not just in operation, but even in theory. There's a long history that goes back to the earliest modern democratic revolutions in seventeenth century England which largely expresses this point of view. I'm just going to keep to the modern period and say a few words about how that notion of democracy develops and why and how the problem of media and disinformation enters within that context.

EARLY HISTORY OF PROPAGANDA

Let's begin with the first modern government propaganda operation. That was under the Woodrow Wilson Administration. Woodrow Wilson was elected President in 1916 on the platform "Peace Without Victory." That was right in the middle of the World War I. The population was extremely pacifistic and saw no reason to become involved in a European war. The Wilson administration was actually committed to war and had to do something about it. They established a government propaganda commission, called the Creel Commission, which succeeded, within six months, in turning a pacifist population into a hysterical, war–mongering population which wanted to destroy everything German, tear the Germans limb from limb, go to war and save the world. That was a major achievement, and it led to a further achievement. Right at that time and after the war the same techniques were used to whip up a hysterical Red Scare, as it was called, which succeeded pretty much in destroying unions and eliminating such dangerous problems as freedom of the press and freedom of political thought. There was very strong support from the media, from the business establishment, which in fact organized, pushed much of this work, and it was, in general, a great success.

Among those who participated actively and enthusiastically in Wilson's war were the progressive intellectuals, people of the John Dewey circle, who took great pride, as you can see from their own writings at the time, in having shown that what they called the "more intelligent members of the community," namely, themselves, were able to drive a reluctant population into a war by terrifying them and eliciting jingoist fanaticism. The means that were used were extensive. For example, there was a good deal of fabrication of atrocities by the Huns, Belgian babies with their arms torn off, all sorts of

NOAM CHOMSKY

awful things that you still read in history books. Much of it was invented by the British propaganda ministry, whose own commitment at the time, as they put it in their secret deliberations, was "to direct the thought of most of the world." But more crucially they wanted to control the thought of the more intelligent members of the community in the United States, who would then disseminate the propaganda that they were concocting and convert the pacifistic country to wartime hysteria. That worked. It worked very well. And it taught a lesson: State propaganda, when supported by the educated classes and when no deviation is permitted from it, can have a big effect. It was a lesson learned by Hitler and many others, and it has been pursued to this day.

Another group that was impressed by these successes was liberal democratic theorists and leading media figures, like, for example, Walter Lippmann, who was the dean of American journalists, a major foreign and domestic policy critic and also a major theorist of liberal democracy. If you take a look at his collected essays, you'll see that they're subtitled something like "A Progressive Theory of Liberal Democratic Thought." Lippmann was involved in these propaganda commissions and recognized their achievements. He argued that what he called a "revolution in the art of democracy," could be used to "manufacture consent, " that is, to bring about agreement on the part of the public for things that they didn't want by the new techniques of propaganda. He also thought that this was a good idea, in fact, necessary. It was necessary because, as he put it, "the common interests elude public opinion entirely" and can only be understood and managed by a "specialized class "of "responsible men" who are smart enough to figure things out. This theory asserts that only a small elite, the intellectual community that the Deweyites were talking about, can understand the common interests, what all of us care about, and that these things "elude the general public." This is a view that goes back hundreds of years. It's also a typical Leninist view. In fact, it has very close resemblance to the Leninist conception that a vanguard of revolutionary intellectuals take state power, using popular revolutions as the force that brings them to state power, and then drive the stupid masses toward a future that they're too dumb and incompetent to envision for themselves. The liberal democratic theory and Marxism–Leninism are very close in their common ideological assumptions. I think that's one reason why people have found it so easy over the years to drift from one position to another without any particular sense of change. It's just a matter of assessing where power is. Maybe there will be a popular revolution, and that will put us into state power; or maybe there won't be, in which case we'll just work for the people with real power: the business community. But we'll do the same thing. We'll drive the stupid masses toward a world that they're too dumb to understand for themselves.

Lippmann backed this up by a pretty elaborated theory of progressive democracy. He argued that in a properly functioning democracy there are classes of citizens. There is first of all the class of citizens who have to take some active role in running general affairs. That's the specialized class. They are the people who analyze, execute, make decisions, and run things in the political, economic, and ideological systems. That's a small percentage of the population. Naturally, anyone who puts these ideas forth is always part of that small group, and they're talking about what to do about *those others*. Those others, who are out of the small group, the big majority of the population, they are what Lippmann called "the bewildered herd." We have to protect ourselves from "the trampling and roar of a bewildered herd". Now there are two "functions" in a democracy: The specialized class, the responsible men, carry out the executive function, which means they do the thinking and planning and understand the common interests. Then, there is the bewildered herd, and they have a function in democracy too. Their function in a democracy, he said, is to be "spectators," not participants in action. But they have more of a function than that, because it's a democracy. Occasionally they are allowed to lend their weight to one or another member of the specialized class. In other words, they're allowed to say, "We want you to be our leader" or "We want *you* to be our leader." That's because it's a democracy and not a totalitarian state. That's called an election. But once they've lent their weight to one or another member of the specialized class they're supposed to sink back and become spectators of action, but not participants. That's in a properly functioning democracy.

And there's a logic behind it. There's even a kind of compelling moral principle behind it. The compelling moral principle is that the mass of the public are just too stupid to be able to understand things. If they try to participate in managing their own affairs, they're just going to cause trouble. Therefore, it would be immoral and improper to permit them to do this. We have to tame the bewildered herd, not allow the bewildered herd to rage and trample and destroy things. It's pretty much the same logic that says that it would be improper to let a three-year-old run across the street. You don't give a three-year-old that kind of freedom because the three-year-old doesn't know how to handle that freedom. Correspondingly, you don't allow the bewildered herd to become participants in action. They'll just cause trouble.

So we need something to tame the bewildered herd, and that something is this new revolution in the art of democracy: the manufacture of consent. The media, the schools, and popular culture have to be divided. For the political class and the decision makers they have to provide them some tolerable sense of reality, although they also have to instill the proper beliefs. Just remember, there is an unstated premise here. The unstated premise —and even the responsible men have to disguise this from themselves—has to do with the question of how they get into the position where they have the authority to make decisions. The way they do that, of course, is by serving people with *real* power. The people with real power are the ones who own the society, which is a pretty narrow group. If the specialized class can come along and say, I can serve your interests, then they'll be part of the executive group. You've got to keep that quiet. That means they have to have instilled in them the beliefs and doctrines that will serve the interests of private power. Unless they can master that skill, they're not part of the specialized class. So we have one kind of educational system directed to the responsible men, the specialized class. They have to be deeply indoctrinated in the values and interests of private power and the state-corporate nexus that represents it. If they can achieve that, then they can be part of the specialized class. The rest of the bewildered herd basically just have to be distracted. Turn their attention to something else. Keep them out of trouble. Make sure that they remain at most spectators of action, occasionally lending their weight to one or another of the real leaders, who they may select among.

This point of view has been developed by lots of other people. In fact, it's pretty conventional. For example, the leading theologian and foreign policy critic Reinhold Niebuhr, sometimes called "the theologian of the establishment," the guru of George Kennan and the Kennedy intellectuals, put it that rationality is a very narrowly restricted skill. Only a small number of people have it. Most people are guided by just emotion and impulse. Those of us who have rationality have to create "necessary illusions" and emotionally potent "oversimplifications" to keep the naïve simpletons more or less on course. This became a substantial part of contemporary political science. In the 1920s and early 1930s, Harold Lasswell, the founder of the modern field of communications and one of the leading American political scientists, explained that we should not succumb to "democratic dogmatisms about men being the best judges of their own interests." Because they're not. We're the best judges of the public interests. Therefore, just out of ordinary morality, we have to make sure that they don't have an opportunity to act on the basis of their misjudgments. In what is nowadays called a totalitarian state, or a military state, it's easy. You just hold a bludgeon over their heads, and if they get out of line you smash them over the head. But as society has become more free and democratic, you lose that capacity. Therefore you have to turn to the techniques of propaganda. The logic is clear. Propaganda is to a democracy what the bludgeon is to a totali-

NOAM CHOMSKY

tarian state. That's wise and good because, again, the common interests elude the bewildered herd. They can't figure them out.

The United States pioneered the public relations industry. Its commitment was "to control the public mind," as its leaders put it. They learned a lot from the successes of the Creel Commission and the successes in creating the Red Scare and its aftermath. The public relations industry underwent a huge expansion at that time. It succeeded for some time in creating almost total subordination of the public to business rule through the 1920s. This was so extreme that Congressional committees began to investigate it as we moved into the 1930s. That's where a lot of our information about it comes from.

Public relations is a huge industry. They're spending by now something on the order of a billion dollars a year. All along its commitment was to *controlling the public mind*. In the 1930s, big problems arose again, as they had during the First World War. There was a huge depression and substantial labor organizing. In fact, in 1935 labor won its first major legislative victory, namely, the right to organize, with the Wagner Act. That raised two serious problems. For one thing, democracy was misfunctioning. The bewildered herd was actually winning legislative victories, and it's not supposed to work that way. The other problem was that it was becoming possible for people to organize. People have to be atomized and segregated and alone. They're not supposed to organize, because then they might be something beyond spectators of action. They might actually be participants if many people with limited resources could get together to enter the political arena. That's really threatening. A major response was taken on the part of business to ensure that this would be the last legislative victory for labor and that it would be the beginning of the end of this democratic deviation of popular organization. It worked. That was the last legislative victory for labor. From that point on—although the number of people in the unions increased for a while during the World War II, after which it started dropping—the capacity to act through the unions began to steadily drop. It wasn't by accident. We're now talking about the business community, which spends lots and lots of money, attention, and thought into how to deal with these problems through the public relations industry and other organizations, like the National Association of Manufacturers and the Business Roundtable, and so on. They immediately set to work to try to find a way to counter these democratic deviations.

The first trial was one year later, in 1937. There was a major strike, the Steel strike in western Pennsylvania at Johnstown. Business tried out a new technique of labor destruction, which worked very well. Not through goon squads and breaking knees. That wasn't working very well any more, but through the more subtle and effective means of propaganda. The idea was to figure out ways to turn the public against the strikers, to present the strikers as disruptive, harmful to the public and against the common interests. The common interests are those of "us," the businessman, the worker, the housewife. That's all "us." We want to be together and have things like harmony and Americanism and working together. Then there's those bad strikers out there who are disruptive and causing trouble and breaking harmony and violating Americanism. We've got to stop them so we can all live together. The corporate executive and the guy who cleans the floors all have the same interests. We can all work together and work for Americanism in harmony, liking each other. That was essentially the message. A huge amount of effort was put into presenting it. This is, after all, the business community, so they control the media and have massive resources. And it worked, very effectively. It was later called the "Mohawk Valley formula" and applied over and over again to break strikes. They were called "scientific methods of strike-breaking," and worked very effectively by mobilizing community opinion in favor of vapid, empty concepts like Americanism. Who can be against that? Or harmony. Who can be against that? Or, as in the Persian Gulf War, "Support our troops." Who can be against that? Or yellow ribbons. Who can be against that? Anything that's totally vacuous.

In fact, what does it mean if somebody asks you, Do you support the people in Iowa? Can you say, Yes, I support them, or No, I don't support them? It's not even a question. It doesn't mean anything.

That's the point. The point of public relations slogans like "Support our troops" is that they don't mean anything. They mean as much as whether you support the people in Iowa. Of course, there was an issue. The issue was, Do you support our policy? But you don't want people to think about that issue. That's the whole point of good propaganda. You want to create a slogan that nobody's going to be against, and everybody's going to be for. Nobody knows what it means, because it doesn't mean anything. Its crucial value is that it diverts your attention from a question that *does* mean something: Do you support our policy? That's the one you're not allowed to talk about. So you have people arguing about support for the troops? "Of course I don't *not* support them." Then you've won. That's like Americanism and harmony. We're all together, empty slogans, let's join in, let's make sure we don't have these bad people around to disrupt our harmony with their talk about class struggle, rights and that sort of business.

That's all very effective. It runs right up to today. And of course it is carefully thought out. The people in the public relations industry aren't there for the fun of it. They're doing work. They're trying to instill the right values. In fact, they have a conception of what democracy ought to be: It ought to be a system in which the specialized class is trained to work in the service of the masters, the people who own the society. The rest of the population ought to be deprived of any form of organization, because organization just causes trouble. They ought to be sitting alone in front of the TV and having drilled into their heads the message, which says, the only value in life is to have more commodities or live like that rich middle class family you're watching and to have nice values like harmony and Americanism. That's all there is in life. You may think in your own head that there's got to be something more in life than this, but since you're watching the tube alone you assume, I must be crazy, because that's all that's going on over there. And since there is no organization permitted—that's absolutely crucial—you never have a way of finding out whether you are crazy, and you just assume it, because it's the natural thing to assume.

So that's the ideal. Great efforts are made in trying to achieve that ideal. Obviously, there is a certain conception behind it. The conception of democracy is the one that I mentioned. The bewildered herd is a problem. We've got to prevent their roar and trampling. We've got to distract them. They should be watching the Superbowl or sitcoms or violent movies. Every once in a while you call on them to chant meaningless slogans like "Support our troops." You've got to keep them pretty scared, because unless they're properly scared and frightened of all kinds of devils that are going to destroy them from outside or inside or somewhere, they may start to think, which is very dangerous, because they're not competent to think. Therefore it's important to distract them and marginalize them.

That's one conception of democracy. In fact, going back to the business community, the last legal victory for labor really was 1935, the Wagner Act. After the war came, the unions declined as did a very rich working class culture that was associated with the unions. That was destroyed. We moved to a business–run society at a remarkable level. This is the only state-capitalist industrial society which doesn't have even the normal social contract that you find in comparable societies. Outside of South Africa, I guess, this is the only industrial society that doesn't have national health care. There's no general commitment to even minimal standards of survival for the parts of the population who can't follow those rules and gain things for themselves individually. Unions are virtually nonexistent. Other forms of popular structure are virtually nonexistent. There are no political parties or organizations. It's a long way toward the ideal, at least structurally. The media are a corporate monopoly. They have the same point of view. The two parties are two factions of the business party. Most of the population doesn't even bother voting because it looks meaningless. They're marginalized and properly distracted. At least that's the goal. The leading figure in the public relations industry, Edward Bernays, actually came out of the Creel Commission. He was part of it, learned his lessons there and went on to develop what he called the "engineering of consent," which he described as "the essence of democracy." The people who are able to engineer consent are the ones who have the resources and the power to do it—the business community—and that's who you work for.

ENGINEERING OPINION

It is also necessary to whip up the population in support of foreign adventures. Usually the population is pacifist, just like they were during the First World War. The public sees no reason to get involved in foreign adventures, killing, and torture. So you *have* to whip them up. And to whip them up you have to frighten them. Bernays himself had an important achievement in this respect. He was the person who ran the public relations campaign for the United Fruit Company in 1954, when the United States moved in to overthrow the capitalist-democratic government of Guatemala and installed a murderous death-squad society, which remains that way to the present day with constant infusions of U.S. aid to prevent in more than empty form democratic deviations. It's necessary to constantly ram through domestic programs which the public is opposed to, because there is no reason for the public to be in favor of domestic programs that are harmful to them. *This*, too, takes extensive propaganda. We've seen a lot of this in the last ten years. The Reagan programs were overwhelmingly unpopular. Voters in the 1984 "Reagan landslide," by about three to two, hoped that his policies would not be enacted. If you take particular programs, like armaments, cutting back on social spending, etc., almost every one of them was overwhelmingly opposed by the public. But as long as people are marginalized and distracted and have no way to organize or articulate their sentiments, or even know that others have these sentiments, people who said that they prefer social spending to military spending, who gave that answer on polls, as people overwhelmingly did, assumed that they were the only people with that crazy idea in their heads. They never heard it from anywhere else. Nobody's supposed to think that. Therefore, if you do think it and you answer it in a poll, you just assume that you're sort of weird. Since there's no way to get together with other people who share or reinforce that view and help you articulate it, you feel like an oddity, an oddball. So you just stay on the side and you don't pay any attention to what's going on. You look at something else, like the Superbowl.

To a certain extent, then, that ideal was achieved, but never completely. There are institutions which it has as yet been impossible to destroy. The churches, for example, still exist. A large part of the dissident activity in the United States comes out of the churches, for the simple reason that they're there. So when you go to a European country and give a political talk, it may very likely be in the union hall. Here that won't happen, because unions first of all barely exist, and if they do exist they're not political organizations. But the churches do exist, and therefore you often give a talk in a church. Central American solidarity work mostly grew out of the churches, mainly because they exist.

The bewildered herd never gets properly tamed, so this is a constant battle. In the 1930s they arose again and were put down. In the 1960s there was another wave of dissidence. There was a name for that. It was called by the specialized class "the crisis of democracy." Democracy was regarded as entering into a crisis in the 1960s. The crisis was that large segments of the population were becoming organized and active and trying to participate in the political arena. Here we come back to these two conceptions of democracy. By the dictionary definition, that's an *advance* in democracy. By the prevailing conception that's a *problem*, a crisis that has to be overcome. The population has to be driven back to the apathy, obedience and passivity that is their proper state. We therefore have to do something to overcome the crisis. Efforts were made to achieve that. It hasn't worked. The crisis of democracy is still alive and well, fortunately, but not very effective in changing policy. But it is effective in changing opinion, contrary to what a lot of people believe. Great efforts were made after the 1960s to try to reverse and overcome this malady. One aspect of the malady actually got a technical name. It was called the "Vietnam Syndrome." The Vietnam Syndrome, a term that began to come up around 1970, has actually been defined on occasion. The Reaganite intellectual Norman Podhoretz defined it as "the sickly inhibitions against the use of military force." There were these sickly inhibitions against violence on the part of a large part of the public.

People just didn't understand why we should go around torturing people and killing people and carpet bombing them. It's very dangerous for a population to be overcome by these sickly inhibitions, as Goebbels understood, because then there's a limit on foreign adventures. It's necessary, as the *Washington Post* put it rather proudly during the Gulf War hysteria, to instill in people respect for "martial value." That's important. If you want to have a violent society that uses force around the world to achieve the ends of its own domestic elite, it's necessary to have a proper appreciation of the martial virtues and none of these sickly inhibitions about using violence. So that's the Vietnam Syndrome. It's necessary to overcome that one.

REPRESENTATION AS REALITY

It's also necessary to completely falsify history. That's another way to overcome these sickly inhibitions, to make it look as if when we attack and destroy somebody we're really protecting and defending ourselves against major aggressors and monsters and so on. There has been a *huge* effort since the Vietnam war to reconstruct the history of that. Too many people began to understand what was really going on. Including plenty of soldiers and a lot of young people who were involved with the peace movement and others. That was bad. It was necessary to rearrange those bad thoughts and to restore some form of sanity, namely, a recognition that whatever we do is noble and right. If we're bombing South

Vietnam, that's because we're defending South Vietnam against somebody, namely, the South Vietnamese, since nobody else was there. It's what the Kennedy intellectuals called defense against "internal aggression" in South Vietnam. That was the phrase used by Adlai Stevenson and others. It was necessary to make that the official and well understood picture. That's worked pretty well. When you have total control over the media and the educational system and scholarship is conformist, you can get that across. One indication of it was revealed in a study done at the University of Massachusetts on attitudes toward the current Gulf crisis—a study of beliefs and attitudes in television watching. One of the questions asked in that study was, How many Vietnamese casualties would you estimate that there were during the Vietnam war? The average response on the part of Americans today is about 100,000. The official figure is about two million. The actual figure is probably three to four million. The people who conducted the study raised an appropriate question: What would we think about German political culture if, when you asked people today how many Jews died in the Holocaust, they estimated about 300,000? What would that tell us about German political culture? They leave the question unanswered, but you can pursue it. What does it tell us about our culture? It tells us quite a bit. It is necessary to overcome the sickly inhibitions against the use of military force and other democratic deviations. In this particular case it worked. This is true on every topic. Pick the topic you like: the Middle East, international terrorism, Central America, whatever it is—the picture of the world that's presented to the public has only the remotest relation to reality. The truth of the matter is buried under edifice after edifice of lies upon lies. It's all been a marvelous success from the point of view in deterring the threat of democracy, achieved under conditions of freedom, which is extremely interesting. It's not like a totalitarian state, where it's done by force. These achievements are under conditions of freedom. If we want to understand our own society, we'll have to think about these facts. They are important facts, important for those who care about what kind of society they live in.

DISSIDENT CULTURE

Despite all of this, the dissident culture survived. It's grown quite a lot since the 1960s. In the 1960s the dissident culture first of all was extremely slow in developing. There was no protest against the Indochina war until years after the United States had started bombing South Vietnam. When it did grow it was a very narrow dissident movement, mostly students and young people. By the 1970s that had changed considerably. Major popular movements had developed: the environmental movement, the feminist movement, the anti-nuclear movement, and others. In the 1980s there was an even greater expansion to the solidarity movements, which is something very new and important in the history of at least American, and maybe even world dissidence. These were movements that not only protested but actually involved themselves, often intimately, in the lives of suffering people elsewhere. They learned a great deal from it and had quite a civilizing effect on mainstream America. All of this has made a very large difference. Anyone who has been involved in this kind of activity for many years must be aware of this. I know myself that the kind of talks I give today in the most reactionary parts of the country—central Georgia, rural Kentucky, etc.—are talks of the kind that I couldn't have given at the peak of the peace movement to the most active peace movement audience. Now you can give them anywhere. People may agree or not agree, but at least they understand what you're talking about and there's some sort of common ground that you can pursue.

These are all signs of the civilizing effect, despite all the propaganda, despite all the efforts to control thought and manufacture consent. Nevertheless, people are acquiring an ability and a willingness to think things through. Skepticism about power has grown, and attitudes have changed on many, many issues. It's kind of slow, maybe even glacial, but perceptible and important. Whether it's fast enough to make a significant difference in what happens in the world is another question. Just to take one familiar example of it: The famous gender gap. In the 1960s attitudes of men and women were approximately the same on such matters as the "martial virtues" and the sickly inhibitions against the use of military force. Nobody, neither men nor women, were suffering from those sickly inhibitions in the early 1960s. The responses were the same. Everybody thought that the use of violence to suppress people out there was just right. Over the years it's changed. The sickly inhibitions have increased all across the board. But meanwhile a gap has been growing, and by now it's a very substantial gap. According to polls, it's something like twenty-five percent. What has happened? What has happened is that there is some form of at least semi-organized popular movement that women are involved in—the feminist movement. Organization has its effects. It means that you discover that you're not alone. Others have the same thoughts that you do. You can reinforce your thoughts and learn more about what you think and believe. These are very informal movements, not like a membership organizations, just a mood that involves inter-actions among people. It has a very noticeable effect. That's the danger of democracy: If organizations can develop, if people are no longer just glued to the tube, you may have all these funny thoughts arising in their heads, like sickly inhibitions against the use of military force. That has to be overcome, but it hasn't been overcome.

PARADE OF ENEMIES

Instead of talking about the last war, let me talk about the next war, because sometimes it's useful to be prepared instead of just reacting. There is a very characteristic development going on in the United States now. It's not the first country in the world that's done this. There are growing domestic social and economic problems, in fact, maybe catastrophes. Nobody in power has any intention of doing anything about them. If you look at the domestic programs of the administrations of the past ten years—I include here the Democratic opposition—there's really no serious proposal about what to do about the severe problems of health, education, homelessness, joblessness, crime, soaring criminal

42

populations, jails, deterioration in the inner cities—
the whole raft of problems. You all know about
them, and they're all getting worse. Just in the two
years that George Bush has been in office three million more children crossed the poverty line, the debt
is zooming, educational standards are declining, real
wages are now back to the level of about the late
1950s for much of the population, and nobody's
doing anything about it. In such circumstances
you've got to divert the bewildered herd, because if
they start noticing this they may not like it, since
they're the ones suffering from it. Just having them
watch the Superbowl and the sitcoms may not be
enough. You have to whip them up into fear of ene-
mies. In the 1930s Hitler whipped them into fear of
the Jews and gypsies. You had to crush them to
defend yourselves. We have our ways, too. Over the
last ten years, every year or two, some major monster is constructed that we have to defend ourselves
against. There used to be one that was always read-
ily available: The Russians. You could always
defend yourself against the Russians. But they're los-
ing their attractiveness as an enemy, and it's getting
harder and harder to use that one, so some new ones
have to be conjured up. In fact, people have quite

unfairly criticized George Bush for being unable to express or articulate what's really driving us now. That's very unfair. Prior to about the mid-1980s, when you were asleep you would just play the record: the Russians are coming. But he lost that one and he's got to make up new ones, just like the Reaganite public relations apparatus did in the 1980s. So it was international terrorists and narco-traffickers and crazed Arabs and Saddam Hussein, the new Hitler, was going to conquer the world. They've got to keep coming up one after another. You frighten the population, terrorize them, intimidate them so that they're too afraid to travel and cower in fear. Then you have a magnificent victory over Grenada, Panama, or some other defenseless third-world army that you can pulverize before you ever bother to look at them—which is just what happened. That gives relief. We were saved at the last minute. That's one of the ways in which you can keep the bewildered herd from paying attention to what's really going on around them, keep them diverted and controlled. The next one that's coming along, most likely, will be Cuba. That's going to require a continuation of the illegal economic warfare, possibly a revival of the extraordinary international terrorism. The most major international terrorism organized yet has been the Kennedy administration's Operation Mongoose, then the things that followed along, against Cuba. There's been nothing remotely comparable to it except perhaps the war against Nicaragua, if you call that terrorism. The World Court classified it as something more like aggression. There's always an ideological offensive that builds up a chimerical monster, then campaigns to have it crushed. You can't go in if they can fight back. That's much too dangerous. But if you are sure that they will be crushed, maybe we'll knock that one off and heave another sigh of relief.

SELECTIVE PERCEPTION

This has been going on for quite a while. In May 1986, the memoirs of the released Cuban prisoner, Armando Valladares, came out. They quickly became a media sensation. I'll give you a couple of quotes. The media described his revelations as "the definitive account of the vast system of torture and prison by which Castro punishes and obliterates political opposition." It was "an inspiring and unforgettable account" of the "bestial prisons," inhuman torture, [and] record of state violence [under] yet another of this century's mass murderers, who we learn, at last, from this book "has created a new despotism that has institutionalized torture as a mechanism of social control" in "the hell that was the Cuba that [Valladares] lived in." That's the *Washington Post* and *New York Times* in repeated reviews. Castro was described as "a dictatorial goon." His atrocities were revealed in this book so conclusively that "only the most light-headed and cold-blooded Western intellectual will come to the tyrant's defense," said the *Washington Post*. Remember, this is the account of what happened to one man. Let's say it's all true. Let's raise no questions about what happened to the one man who says he was tortured. At a White House ceremony marking Human Rights Day, he was singled out by Ronald Reagan for his courage in enduring the horrors and sadism of this bloody Cuban tyrant. He was then appointed the U.S. representative at the U.N. Human Rights Commission, where he has been able to perform signal services defending the Salvadoran and Guatemalan governments against charges that they conduct atrocities so massive that they make anything he suffered look pretty minor. That's the way things stand.

That was May 1986. It was interesting, and it tells you something about the manufacture of consent. The same month, the surviving members of the Human Rights Group of El Salvador—the leaders had been killed—were arrested and tortured, including Herbert Anaya, who was the director. They were sent to a prison—La Esperanza (hope) Prison. While they were in prison they continued their human rights work. They were lawyers, they continued taking affidavits. There were 432 prisoners in that prison. They got signed affidavits from 430 of them in which they described, under oath, the torture that they had received: electrical torture and other atrocities, including, in one case, torture by a North American U.S. major in uniform, who is described in some detail. This is an unusually explicit and comprehensive testimony, probably unique in its detail about what's going on in a torture chamber. This 160–page report of the prisoners' sworn testimony was sneaked out of prison, along with a videotape which was taken showing people testifying in prison about their torture. It was distributed by the Marin County Interfaith Task Force. *The national press refused to cover it. The TV stations refused to run it.* There was an article in the local Marin County newspaper, the *San Francisco Examiner,* and I think that's all. No one else would touch it. This was a time when there was more than a few "light-headed and cold-blooded Western intellectuals" who were singing the praises of José Napoleón Duarte and of Ronald Reagan. Anaya was not the subject of any tributes. He didn't get on Human Rights Day. He wasn't appointed to anything. He was released in a prisoner exchange and then assassinated, apparently by the U.S.-backed security forces. Very little information about that ever appeared. The media never asked whether exposure of the atrocities—instead of sitting on them and silencing them—might have saved his life.

This tells you something about the way a well-functioning system of consent manufacturing works. In comparison with the revelations of Herbert Anaya in El Salvador, Valladares's memoirs are not even a pea next to the mountain. But you've got your job to do. That takes us toward the next war. I expect, we're going to hear more and more of this, until the next operation takes place.

A few remarks about the last one. Let's turn finally to that. Let me begin with this University of Massachusetts study that I mentioned before. It has some interesting conclusions. In the study people were asked whether they thought that the United States should intervene with force to reverse illegal occupation or serious human rights abuses. By about two to one, people in the United States thought we should. We should use force in the case of illegal occupation of land and *severe* human rights abuses. If the United States was to follow that advice, we would bomb El Salvador, Guatemala, Indonesia, Damascus, Tel Aviv, Capetown, Turkey, Washington, and a whole list of other states. These are all cases of illegal occupation and aggression and severe human rights abuses. If you know the facts about that range of examples, you'll know very well that Saddam Hussein's aggression and atrocities fall well within the range. They're not the most extreme. Why doesn't anybody come to that conclusion? The reason is that nobody knows. In a well-functioning propaganda system, nobody would know what I'm talking about when I list that range of examples. If you bother to look, you find that those examples are quite appropriate.

Take one that was ominously close to being perceived during the Gulf War. In February, right in the middle of the bombing campaign, the government of Lebanon requested Israel to observe U.N. Security Council Resolution 425, which called on it to withdraw immediately and unconditionally from Lebanon. That resolution dates from March

NOAM CHOMSKY

1978. There have since been two subsequent resolutions calling for the immediate and uncondi-
tional withdrawal of Israel from Lebanon. Of course
it doesn't observe them because the United States
backs it in maintaining that occupation. Meanwhile southern Lebanon is terrorized. There are big
torture-chambers with horrifying things going on.
It's used as a base for attacking other parts of
Lebanon. Since 1978, Lebanon was invaded, the
city of Beirut was bombed, about 20,000 people
were killed, about 80 percent of them civilians,
hospitals were destroyed, and more terror, looting,
and robbery was inflicted. All fine, the United
States backed it. That's just one case. You didn't see
anything in the media about it or any discussion
about whether Israel and the United States should
observe U.N. Security Council Resolution 425 or
any of the other resolutions, nor did anyone call for
the bombing of Tel Aviv, although by the principles upheld by two-thirds of the population, we
should. After all, that's illegal occupation and
severe human rights abuses. That's just one case.
There are much worse ones. The Indonesian invasion of East Timor knocked off about 200,000 people. They all look minor by that one. That was

strongly backed by the United States and is *still* going on with major United States diplomatic and military support. We can go on and on.

That tells you how a well-functioning propaganda system works. People can believe that when we use force against Iraq and Kuwait it's because we really observe the principle that illegal occupation and human rights abuses should be met by force. They don't see what it would mean if those principles were applied to U.S. behavior. That's a success of propaganda of quite a spectacular type.

Let's take a look at another case. If you look closely at the coverage of the war since August (1990), you'll notice that there are a couple of striking voices missing. For example, there is an Iraqi democratic opposition, in fact, a very courageous and quite substantial Iraqi democratic opposition.

They, of course, function in exile because they couldn't survive in Iraq. They are in Europe primarily. They are bankers, engineers, architects—people like that. They are articulate, they have voices, and they speak. The previous February, when Saddam Hussein was still George Bush's favorite friend and trading partner, they actually came to Washington, according to Iraqi democratic opposition sources, with a plea for some kind of support for a demand of theirs calling for a parliamentary democracy in Iraq. They were totally rebuffed, because the United States had no interest in it. There was no reaction to this in the public record.

Since August it became a little harder to ignore their existence. In August we suddenly turned against Saddam Hussein after having favored him for many years. Here was an Iraqi democratic opposition who ought to have some thoughts about the matter. They would be happy to see Saddam Hussein drawn and quartered. He killed their brothers, tortured their sisters, and drove them out of the country. They have been fighting against his tyranny throughout the whole time that Ronald Reagan and George Bush were cherishing him. What about their voices? Take a look at the national media

NOAM CHOMSKY

and see how much you can find about the Iraqi democratic opposition from August through March (1991). You can't find a word. It's not that they're inarticulate. They have statements, proposals, calls and demands. If you look at them, you find that they're indistinguishable from those of the American peace movement. They're against Saddam Hussein and they're against the war against Iraq. They don't want their country destroyed. What they want is a peaceful resolution, and they knew perfectly well that it might have been achievable. That's the wrong view and therefore they're out. We don't hear a word about the Iraqi democratic opposition. If you want to find out about them, pick up the German press, or the British press. They don't say much about them, but they're less controlled than we are and they say something.

This is a spectacular achievement of propaganda. First, that the voices of the Iraqi democrats are completely excluded, and second, that nobody notices it. That's interesting, too. It takes a really deeply indoctrinated population not to notice that we're not hearing the voices of the Iraqi democratic opposition and not asking the question, Why? and finding out the obvious answer: because the Iraqi democrats have their own thoughts; they agree with the international peace movement and therefore they're out.

Let's take the question of the reasons for the war. Reasons were offered for the war. The reasons are: aggressors cannot be rewarded and aggression must be reversed by the quick resort to violence; that was the reason for the war. There was basically no other reason advanced. Can that possibly be the reason for the war? Does the United States uphold those principles, that aggressors cannot be rewarded and that aggression must be reversed by a quick resort to violence? I won't insult your intelligence by running through the facts, but the fact is those arguments could be refuted in two minutes by a literate teenager. However, they never were refuted. Take a look at the media, the liberal commentators and critics, the people who testified in Congress and see whether anybody questioned the assumption that the United States stands up to those principles. Has the United States opposed its own aggression in Panama and insisted on bombing Washington to reverse it? When the South African occupation of Namibia was declared illegal in 1969, did the United States impose sanctions on food and medicine? Did it go to war? Did it bomb Capetown? No, it carried out twenty years of "quiet diplomacy." It wasn't very pretty during those twenty years. In the years of the Reagan-Bush administration alone, about 1.5 million people were killed by South Africa just in the surrounding countries. Forget what was happening in South Africa and Namibia. Somehow that didn't sear our sensitive souls. We continued with "quite diplomacy" and ended up with ample reward for the aggressors. They were given the major port in Namibia and plenty of advantages that took into account their security concerns. Where is this principle that we uphold? Again, it's child's play to demonstrate that those couldn't possibly have been the reasons for going to war, because we don't uphold these principles. But nobody did it—that's what's important. And nobody bothered to point out the conclusion that follows: No reason was given for going to war. None. No reason was given for going to war that could not be refuted by a literate teenager in about two minutes. That again is the hallmark of a totalitarian culture. It ought to frighten us, that we are so deeply totalitarian that we can be driven to war without any reason being given for it and without anybody noticing Lebanon's request or caring. It's a very striking fact.

Right before the bombing started, in mid-January, a major *Washington Post*-ABC poll revealed something interesting. People were asked, If Iraq would agree to withdraw from Kuwait in return for Security Council consideration of the problem of Arab-Israeli conflict, would you be in favor of that? By about two-to-one, the population was in favor of that. So was the whole world, including the Iraqi democratic opposition. So it was reported that two-thirds of the American population were in favor of that. Presumably, the people who were in favor of that thought they were the only ones in the world to think so. Certainly nobody in the press had said that it would be a good idea. The orders from Washington have been, we're supposed to be against "linkage," that is, diplomacy, and therefore everybody goose-stepped on command and everybody was against diplomacy. Try to find commentary in the press—you can find a column by Alex Cockburn in the *Los Angeles Times*, who argued that it would be a good idea. The people who were answering that question thought, I'm alone, but that's what I think. Suppose they knew that they weren't alone, that other people thought it, like the Iraqi democratic opposition. Suppose that they knew that this was not hypothetical, that in fact Iraq had made exactly such an offer. It had been released by high U.S. officials just eight days earlier. On January 2, these officials had released an Iraqi offer to withdraw totally from Kuwait in return for consideration by the Security Council of the Arab-Israeli conflict and the problem of weapons of mass destruction. The United States had been refusing to negotiate this issue since well before the invasion of Kuwait. Suppose that people had known that the offer was actually on the table and that it was widely supported and that in fact it's exactly the kind of thing that any rational person would do if they were interested in peace, as we do in other cases, in the rare cases that we do want to reverse aggression. Suppose that it had been known. You can make your own guesses, but I would assume that the two-thirds would probably have risen to 98 percent of the population. Here you have the great successes of propaganda. Probably not one person who answered the poll knew any of the things I've just mentioned. The people thought they were alone. Therefore it was possible to proceed with the war policy without opposition.

There was a good deal of discussion about whether sanctions would work. You had the head of the CIA come up and discuss whether sanctions would work. However, there was no discussion of a much more obvious question: Had sanctions already worked? The answer is yes, apparently they had—probably by late August, very likely by late December. It was very hard to think up any other reason for the Iraqi offers of withdrawal, which were authenticated or in some cases released by high U.S. officials, who described them as "serious" and "negotiable." So the real question is: Had sanctions already worked? Was there a way out? Was there a way out in terms quite acceptable to the general population, the world at large and the Iraqi democratic opposition? These questions were not discussed, and it's crucial for a well-functioning propaganda system that they *not* be discussed. That enables the chairman of the Republican National Committee to say that if any Democrat had been in office, Kuwait would not be liberated today. He can say that and no Democrat would get up and say that if I were president it would have been liberated not only today but six months ago, because there were opportunities then that I would have pursued and Kuwait would have been liberated without killing tens of thousands of people and without causing an environmental catastrophe. No Democrat would say that because no Democrat took that position. Henry Gonzalez and Barbara Boxer took that position. But the number of people who took it is so marginal that it's virtually nonexistent. Given the fact that almost no Democratic politician would say that, Clayton Yeutter is free to make his statements.

When Scud missiles hit Israel, nobody in the press applauded. Again, that's an interesting fact about a well-functioning propaganda system. We might ask, why not? After all, Saddam Hussein's arguments were as good as George Bush's arguments. What were they, after all? Let's just take Lebanon. Saddam Hussein says that he can't stand annexation. He can't let Israel annex the Syrian Golan Heights and East Jerusalem, in opposition to the unanimous agreement of the Security Council. He can't stand annexation. He can't stand aggression. Israel has been occupying southern Lebanon since 1978 in violation of Security Council resolutions that it refuses to abide by. In the course of that period it attacked all of Lebanon, still bombs most of Lebanon at will. He can't stand it. He might have read the Amnesty International report on Israeli atrocities in the West Bank. His heart is bleeding. He can't stand it. Sanctions can't work because the United States vetoes them. Negotiations won't work because the United States blocks them. What's left but force? He's been waiting for years. Thirteen years in the case of Lebanon, 20 years in the case of the West Bank. You've heard that argument before. The only difference between that argument and the one you heard is that Saddam Hussein could truly say sanctions and negotiations can't work because the United States blocks them. But George Bush couldn't say that, because sanctions apparently had worked, and there was every reason to believe that negotiations could work—except that he adamantly refused to pursue them, saying explicitly, there will be no negotiations right through. Did you find anybody in the press who pointed that out? No. It's a triviality. It's something that, again, a literate teenager could figure out in a minute. But nobody pointed it out, no commentator, no editorial writer. That, again, is the sign of a very well-run totalitarian culture. It shows that the manufacture of consent is working.

Last comment about this. We could give many examples, you could make them up as you go along. Take the idea that Saddam Hussein is a monster about to conquer the world—widely believed, in the United States, and not unrealistically. It was drilled into people's heads over and over again: He's about to take everything. We've got to stop him now. How did he get that powerful? This is a small, third-world country without an industrial base. For eight years Iraq had been fighting Iran. That's post-revolutionary Iran, which had decimated its officer corps and most of its military force. Iraq had a little bit of support in that war. It was backed by the Soviet Union, the United States, Europe, the major Arab countries, and the Arab oil producers. It couldn't defeat Iran. But all of a sudden it's ready to conquer the world. Did you find anybody who pointed that out? The fact of the matter is, this was a third-world country with a peasant army. It is now being conceded that there was a ton of disinformation about the fortifications, the chemical weapons, etc. But did you find anybody who pointed it out? No. You found virtually nobody who pointed it out. That's typical. Notice that this was done one year after exactly the same thing was done with Manuel Noriega. Manuel Noriega is a minor thug by comparison with George Bush's friend Saddam Hussein or George Bush's other friends in Beijing or George Bush himself, for that matter. In comparison with them, Manuel Noriega is a pretty minor thug. Bad, but not a world-class thug of the kind we like. He was turned into a creature larger than life. He was going to destroy us, leading the narco-traffickers. We had to quickly move in and smash him, killing a couple hundred or maybe thousand people, restoring to power the tiny, maybe eight percent white oligarchy, and putting U.S. military officers in control at every level of the political system. We had to do all those things because, after all, we had to save ourselves or we were going to be destroyed by this monster. One year later the same thing was done by Saddam Hussein. Did anybody point it out? Did anybody point out what had happened or why? You'll have to look pretty hard for that.

Notice that this is not all that different from what the Creel Commission when it turned a pacifistic population into raving hysterics who wanted to destroy everything German to save ourselves from Huns who were tearing the arms off Belgian babies. The techniques are maybe more sophisticated, with television and lots of money going into it, but it's pretty traditional.

I think the issue, to come back to my original comment, is not simply disinformation and the Gulf crisis. The issue is much broader. It's whether we want to live in a free society or whether we want to live under what amounts to a form of self-imposed totalitarianism, with the bewildered herd marginalized, directed elsewhere, terrified, screaming patriotic slogans, fearing for their lives and admiring with awe the leader who saved them from destruction, while the educated masses goose-step on command and repeat the slogans they're supposed to repeat and the society deteriorates at home. We end up serving as a mercenary enforcer state, hoping that others are going to pay us to smash up the world. Those are the choices. That's the choice that you have to face. The answer to those questions is very much in the hands of people like *you* and *me*.

THE JOURNALIST FROM MARS

How the "War on Terror" Should Be Reported

The following text is an edited transcript of a talk given at Fairness and Accuracy in Reporting's fifteenth anniversary celebration at Town Hall, New York City, January 22, 2002.

THE PROPER TOPIC FOR an occasion like this, I suppose, is pretty obvious: It would be the question of how the media have handled the major story of the past months, the issue of the "war on terrorism," so-called, specifically in the Islamic world. Incidentally, by media here I intend the term to be understood pretty broadly, including journals of commentary, analysis, and opinion; in fact, the intellectual culture generally.

It's a really important topic. It's been reviewed regularly by FAIR, among others. However, it isn't really an appropriate topic for a talk, and the reason is that it requires too much detailed analysis. So what I'd like to do is take a somewhat different approach to it and ask the question of how should the story be handled, in accord with general principles that are accepted as guidelines: principles of fairness, accuracy, relevance, and so on.

Let's approach this by kind of a thought experiment. Imagine an intelligent Martian—I'm told that by convention, Martians are males, so I'll refer to it as "he." Suppose that this Martian went to Harvard and Columbia Journalism School and learned all kinds of high-minded things, and actually believes them. How would the Martian handle a story like this?

I think he would begin with some factual observations that he'd send back to the journal on Mars. One factual observation is that the war on terrorism was not declared on September 11; rather, it was redeclared, using the same rhetoric as the first declaration twenty years earlier. The Reagan administration, as you know, I'm sure, came into office announcing that a war on terrorism would be the core of U.S. foreign policy, and it condemned what the president called the "evil scourge of terrorism."[1] The main focus was state-supported international terrorism in the Islamic world, and at that time also in Central America. International

NOAM CHOMSKY

terrorism was described as a plague spread by "depraved opponents of civilization itself," in "a return to barbarism in the modern age."[2] Actually, I'm quoting the administration moderate, Secretary of State George Shultz.

The phrase I quoted from Reagan had to do with terrorism in the Middle East, and it was the year 1985. That was the year in which international terrorism in that region was selected by editors as the lead story of the year in an annual Associated Press poll, so point one that our Martian would report is that the year 2001 is the second time that this has been the main lead story, and that the war on terrorism has been redeclared pretty much as before.

Furthermore, there's a striking continuity; the same people are in leading positions. So Donald Rumsfeld is running the military component of the second phase of the war on terrorism, and he was Reagan's special envoy to the Middle East during the first phase of the war on terrorism, including the peak year, 1985. The person who was just appointed a couple of months ago to be in charge of the diplomatic component of the war at the United Nations is John Negroponte, who during the first phase was supervising U.S. operations in Honduras, which was the main base for the U.S. war against terror in the first phase.

Exercising the Power Element

In 1985, terrorism in the Middle East was the lead story, but terrorism in Central America had second rank as the story of the day. Shultz, in fact, regarded the plague in Central America as what he called the most alarming manifestation of it. The main problem, he explained, was "a cancer right here in our hemisphere,"[3] and we want to cut it out and we'd better do it fast because the cancer was openly proclaiming the goals of Hitler's *Mein Kampf* and was just about to take over the world. And it was really dangerous. The danger was so severe that on Law Day 1985, the president announced a state of national emergency because of, as he put it, "the unusual and extraordinary threat to the national security and foreign policy of the United States" posed by this cancer. (Law Day, incidentally, is the day that in the rest of the world is commemorated as a day in solidarity with the struggles of American workers. In the United States it's a jingoist holiday, May 1.)

This state of emergency was renewed annually until finally the cancer was cut out. Secretary of

State Shultz explained that the danger was so severe that you can't keep to gentle means; in his words (April 14, 1986), "Negotiations are a euphemism for capitulation if the shadow of power is not cast across the bargaining table." He condemned those who "seek utopian legalistic means like outside mediation, the United Nations, and the World Court while ignoring the power element of the equation."

The United States had been, in fact, exercising the power element of the equation with mercenary forces based in Honduras, under the supervision of John Negroponte, while it was successfully blocking pursuit of utopian legalistic means by the World Court, the Latin American countries, and of course the cancer itself, bent on world conquest.

The media agreed. The only question that arose, really, was tactics. There was the usual hawk/dove debate. The position of the hawks was expressed pretty well by the editors of *The New Republic* (April 4, 1984). They demanded, in their words, that we continue to send military aid to "Latin-style fascists...regardless of how many are murdered," because "there are higher American priorities than Salvadoran human rights," or anywhere else in the region. That's the hawks.

The doves argued, on the other hand, that these means were just not going to work, and they proposed alternative means to return Nicaragua, the cancer, to the "Central American mode" and impose "regional standards" on it. I'm quoting the *Washington Post* (March 14, 1986; March 19, 1986). The Central American mode and the regional standards were those of the terror states El Salvador and Guatemala, which were at that time massacring, torturing, and devastating in ways I don't have to describe. So we had to return Nicaragua to the Central American mode as well, according to the doves.

The op-eds and editorials in the national press were divided on this roughly fifty-fifty between the hawks and the doves. There were exceptions, but they're literally at the level of statistical error. There's material on this in print, and there has been for a long time if you want to take a look.[4] In the other major region where the plague was raging at that time, in the Middle East, uniformity was even more extreme.

Same War, Different targets

Well, the intelligent Martian would certainly pay great attention to all of this very recent history, in fact with remarkable continuity, so that the front pages on Mars would report that the so-called war on terror is redeclared by the same people against rather similar targets, although, he would point out, not quite the same targets.

The depraved opponents of civilization itself in the year 2001 were in the 1980s the freedom fighters organized and armed by the CIA and its associates, trained by the same special forces who are now searching for them in caves in Afghanistan. They were a component of the first war against terror and acting pretty much the same way as the other components of the war against terror.

They didn't hide their terrorist agenda that began early on, in fact in 1981, when they assassinated the President of Egypt, and is continuing. That included terrorist attacks inside Russia severe enough so that at one point they virtually led to a war with Pakistan, although these attacks stopped after the Russians withdrew from Afghanistan in 1989, leaving the ravaged country in the hands of the U.S. favorites, who turned at once to mass murder, rape, terror—generally described as the worst period in Afghanistan's history. They're now back in charge outside of Kabul. According to this morning's *Wall*

Street Journal (January 22, 2001), two of the major warlords are now approaching what could turn out to be a major war. Let's hope not.

All of this is headline news in the Martian press—along, of course, with what it all means to the civilian population. That includes vast numbers of people who are still deprived of desperately needed food and other supplies, although food has been available for months but can't be distributed because of conditions; that's after four months.

The consequences of that we don't know, and in fact will never know. Because there's a principle of the intellectual culture that although you investigate enemy crimes with laserlike intensity, you never look at your own—that's quite important—so we can only give very vague estimates of the number of Vietnamese or Salvadoran or other corpses that we've left around.

The Heresy of Moral Equivalence

As I say, this would be headlines on Mars. A good Martian reporter would also want to clarify a couple of basic ideas. First of all, he'd like to know what exactly is terrorism. And, secondly, what's the proper response to it. Well, whatever the answer to the second question is, that proper response must satisfy some moral truisms, and the Martian can easily discover what these truisms are, at least as understood by the leaders of the self-declared war on terrorism, because they tell us, they tell us constantly, that they are very pious Christians, who therefore revere the Gospels, and have certainly memorized the definition of "hypocrite" given prominently in the Gospels—namely, the hypocrites are those who apply to others the standards that they refuse to accept for themselves.

So the Martian understands, then, that in order to rise to the absolutely minimal moral level we have to agree, in fact insist, that if some act is right for us then it's right for others, and if it's wrong when others do it then it's wrong when we do it. Now that's the most elementary of moral truisms, and once the Martian realizes that, he can pack up his bags and go back to Mars. Because his research task is over. He would be unlikely to find a phrase, a single phrase in the vast coverage and commentary about the war on terrorism that even begins to approach this minimal standard. Don't take my word for it; try the experiment. I don't want to exaggerate—you can probably find the phrase now and then, way out at the margins, though very rarely.

Nevertheless, this moral truism is recognized within the mainstream. It's understood to be an extremely dangerous heresy, and therefore it's necessary to erect impregnable barriers against it, even before anybody exhibits it, even though it's so rare. In fact, there's even a technical vocabulary available in case anybody would dare to engage in the heresy, to involve themselves in the heresy that we should abide by moral truisms that we pretend to revere. The offenders are guilty of something called moral relativism—that means the suggestion that we apply to ourselves the standards we apply to others. Or maybe moral equivalence, which is a term that was invented, I think, by Jeane Kirkpatrick to ward off the danger that somebody might dare to look at our own crimes.

Or maybe they're carrying out the crime of America-bashing, or they're anti-Americans. Which is a rather interesting concept. The term is used elsewhere only in totalitarian states, for example in Russia in the old days, where anti-Sovietism was the highest crime. If somebody were to publish a book in Italy, say, called *The Anti-Italians*, you can imagine what the reaction would be in the streets of Milan and Rome, or in any country where freedom and democracy were taken seriously.

An Unusable Definition

But let's suppose that the Martian isn't deterred by the inevitable tirades and stream of vilification, and suppose he persists in keeping to the most elementary moral truisms. Well, as I said, if he does that, he can just go home, but suppose out of curiosity he decides to stay on and look a little bit further. So, what will happen? Well, back to the question, what is terrorism?—an important one.

There is a proper course for a serious Martian reporter to follow to find the answer to that: Look at the people who declared the war on terrorism and see what they say terrorism is; that's fair enough. And there is in fact an official definition in the U.S. code and Army manuals, and elsewhere. It is defined briefly. Terrorism, as I'm quoting, is defined as "the calculated use of violence or the threat of violence to attain goals that are political, religious or ideological in nature...through intimidation, coercion or instilling fear." Well, that sounds simple; as far as I can see, it's appropriate. But we constantly read that the problem of defining terrorism is very vexing and complex, and the Martian might wonder why that's true. And there's an answer.

The official definition is unusable. It's unusable for two important reasons. First of all, it's a very close paraphrase of official government policy—very close, in fact. When it's government policy, it's called low-intensity conflict or counterterror.

Incidentally, it's not just the United States. As far as I'm aware, this practice is universal. Just as an example, back in the mid 1960s the Rand Corporation, the research agency connected with the Pentagon mostly, published a collection of interesting Japanese counterinsurgency manuals having to do with the Japanese attack on Manchuria and North China in the 1930s. I was kind of interested—I wrote an article on it at the time comparing the Japanese counterinsurgency manuals with U.S. counterinsurgency manuals for South Vietnam, which are virtually identical.[5] That article didn't fly too well, I should say.

Well, anyhow, it's a fact, and as far as I know it's a universal fact. So that's one reason you can't use the official definition. The other reason you can't do it is much simpler: it just gives all the wrong answers, radically so, as to who the terrorists are.

So therefore the official definition has to be abandoned, and you have to search for some kind of sophisticated definition that will give the right answers, and that's hard. That's why you hear that it's such a difficult topic and big minds are wrestling with it and so on.

Fortunately, there is a solution. The solution is to define terrorism as the terrorism that they carry out against us, whoever we happen to be. As far as I know, that's universal—in journalism, in scholarship, and also I think it's a historical universal; at least, I've never found any country that doesn't follow this practice. So, fortunately, there's a way out of the problem. Well, with this useful characterization of terrorism, we can then draw the standard conclusions that you read all the time: namely, that we and our allies are the main victims of terrorism, and that terrorism is a weapon of the weak.

Of course, terrorism in the official sense is a weapon of the strong, like most weapons, but it's a weapon of the weak, by definition, once you comprehend that "terrorism" just means the terrorism that they carry out against us. Then of course it's true by definition that terrorism is a weapon of the weak. And so the people who write it all the time, you see it in the newspapers or the journals, they're right; it's a tautology, and by convention.

Textbook Terrorism

Suppose the Martian goes on to defy what are apparently universal conventions, and he actually accepts the moral truisms that are preached and he also even accepts the official U.S. definition of terrorism. I should say that by this time he's way out in outer space, but let's proceed. If he goes this far, then there certainly are clear illustrations of terrorism. September 11, for example, is a particularly shocking example of a terrorist atrocity. Another equally clear example is the official U.S.-British reaction, which was announced by Admiral Sir Michael Boyce, chief of the British defense staff, and reported in a front- page story in the *New York Times* in late October (October 28, 2001). He informed the people of Afghanistan that the United States and Britain would continue their attack against them "until they get the leadership changed."

Notice that this is a textbook illustration of international terrorism, according to the official definition; I won't reread it but if you think about it, it's just a perfect illustration.

NOAM CHOMSKY

Two weeks before that, George Bush had informed the Afghans, the people of Afghanistan, that the attack will go on until they hand over wanted suspects. Remember that overthrow of the Taliban regime was a sort of afterthought brought in a couple of weeks after the bombing, basically for the benefit of intellectuals so they could write about how just the war is.

This of course was also textbook terrorism: We're going to continue to bomb you until you hand over some people we want you to hand over. The Taliban regime did ask for evidence, but the U.S. contemptuously dismissed that request. The U.S., at the very same time, also flatly refused to even consider offers of extradition, which may have been serious, may not have been; we don't know because they were rejected.

The Martian would certainly record all of this, and if he did a little homework he would quickly find the reasons, adding many other examples. The reasons are very simple: The world's rulers have to make it clear that they do not defer to any authority. Therefore they do not accept the idea that they should offer evidence, they do not agree that they should request extradition; in fact, they reject UN

Security Council authorization, reject it flatly. The U.S. could easily have obtained clear and unambiguous authorization—not for pretty reasons, but it could have obtained it. However, it rejected that option.

And that makes good sense. In fact, there's even a term for this in the literature of international affairs and diplomacy. It's called establishing credibility. Another term for it is declaring that we're a terrorist state and you'd better be aware of the consequences if you get in our way. Now that's, of course, only if we use "terrorism" in its official sense, as it's defined in U.S. government legal code and so on, and that's unacceptable for reasons that I mentioned.

Uncontroversial Cases

Let's go back to the moral truism. According to official doctrine, which is almost universally accepted and described as just and admirable and obviously so, the United States is entitled to conduct a terrorist war against Afghans until they hand over suspects to the United States, which refuses to provide evidence or request extradition, or, in Boyce's later terms, until they change their leadership. Well, anyone who is not a hypocrite in the sense of the Gospels will therefore conclude at once that Haiti is entitled to carry out large-scale terrorism against the United States until it hands over a murderer, Emmanuel Constant, who has already been convicted of leading the terrorist forces that had the major responsibility for four to five thousand deaths.

No question about the evidence in this case. They've requested extradition repeatedly, most recently on September 30, 2001, right in the midst of all the talk about Afghanistan being subjected to terrorism if it doesn't hand over suspected terrorists. Of course, that's only four or five thousand black people. I guess it doesn't count quite as much.

Or perhaps they should carry out massive terror in the United States. Since they can't bomb, maybe bioterror or something, I don't know, until the United States changes its leadership, which is, in fact, responsible for terrible crimes against the people of Haiti right through the twentieth century.

Or certainly, keeping now to moral truisms, Nicaragua is entitled to do the same, incidentally targeting the leaders of the redeclared war on ter-

rorism, the same people often. Recall that the terrorist attack against Nicaragua was far more severe
than even September 11; tens of thousands of people were killed, the country was devastated, it may
never recover.

Also, this happens to be an uncontroversial
example, so we don't have to argue about it. It's
uncontroversial because of the judgment of the
World Court condemning the United States for
international terrorism, backed up by the Security
Council in a resolution calling on all states to
observe international law—mentioning no one, but
everyone knew who they meant—vetoed by the
United States, Britain abstaining. Or the judgment
of the General Assembly in successive resolutions
confirming the same thing, opposed by the United
States and one or two client states. The World
Court ordered the United States to terminate the
crime of international terrorism, to pay massive
reparations. The U.S. responded with a bipartisan
decision to escalate the attack immediately; I
already described the media reaction. All of this
continued until the cancer was destroyed and it
continues right now.

So in November 2001 there was an election in

NOAM CHOMSKY

Nicaragua, right in the middle of the war on terrorism, and the United States radically intervened in the election. It warned Nicaragua that the United States would not accept the wrong outcome, and even gave the reason. The State Department explained that we cannot overlook Nicaragua's role in international terrorism in the 1980s, when it resisted the international terrorist attack that led to the condemnation of the United States for international terrorism by the highest international authorities.

Here all of this passes without comment in an intellectual culture that is simply dedicated passionately to terrorism and hypocrisy, but I guess it might have had some headlines in the Martian press. You might look and see how it was treated here. You might also incidentally try out your favorite theory of "just war" in this uncontroversial case.

Domesticating the Majority

Nicaragua, of course, had some defense against the U.S.-run international terrorism being carried out against it under the pretext of a war on terrorism. Namely, Nicaragua had an army. In the other Central American countries, the terrorist forces that were armed and trained by the U.S. and its clients were the army, so not surprisingly the terrorist atrocities were far worse. That's the Central American mode that the doves said we have to return the cancer to. But in this case the victims weren't the state, and therefore they could not appeal to the World Court or to the Security Council for judgments that would be rejected, tossed into the ashcan of history, except maybe on Mars.

The effects of that terror were long-lasting. Here in the United States, there's a good deal of concern—very properly as a matter of fact—about the very wide-ranging effects of the terrorist atrocities of September 11. So, for example, there's a front-page article in the *New York Times* (January 22, 2002) about the people who are beyond the reach of benefits for the tragedy that they suffered. Of course, the same is true for those who are victims of vastly worse terrorist crimes, but that's reported only on Mars.

So you might try to find the report, say, of a conference run by Salvadoran Jesuits a couple of years ago. The Jesuits' experiences under U.S. international terrorism were particularly grisly. The conference report[6] stressed the residual effect of what it called the culture of terrorism, which domesticates the aspirations of the majority, who realized that they must submit to the dictates of the ruling terrorist state and its local agents or they will again be returned to the Central American mode, as recommended by the doves at the peak of the state-supported international terrorism of the eightees. Unreported here, of course; maybe headlines on Mars.

Enthusiastic Partners

Actually, the Martian might notice some other interesting similarities between the first and the second phase of the war on terror. In the year 2001, just about every terrorist state you think of was eagerly joining in the coalition against terrorism, and the reasons are not hidden.

We all know why the Russians are so enthusiastic: they want U.S. endorsement for their monstrous terrorist activities in Chechnya, for example.

Turkey was particularly enthusiastic. They were the first country to offer troops, and the prime minister explained why. This was in gratitude for the fact that the United States alone was willing to pour arms into Turkey—providing eighty percent of their arms in the Clinton years—in order to enable them to expedite some of the worst terrorist atrocities and ethnic cleansing of the 1990s. And they're very grateful for that, and so they offered troops for the new war on terrorism. Incidentally, none of this counts as terrorism, remember, because by the convention, since we're carrying it out it's not terrorism. And so on down the list; I won't go through the rest.

And the same, incidentally, was true of the first phase of the war on terrorism. So the announcement by Admiral Boyce that I quoted was a close paraphrase of words of the well-known Israeli statesman Abba Eban in 1981. That was shortly after the first war against terrorism was declared. Eban was justifying Israeli atrocities in Lebanon, which he acknowledged were pretty awful, but justified, he said, because "there was a rational prospect that affected populations would exert pressure for a cessation of hostilities."[7] Notice that's another textbook illustration of international terrorism in the official sense.

The hostilities that he was talking about were at the Israel-Lebanon border, overwhelmingly Israeli in origin, often without even a pretext, but backed by the United States, so therefore they're not terrorism by convention and they're not part of the history of terrorism. At the time, with decisive U.S. support,

Israel was carrying out attacks in Lebanon, bombing and other atrocities, to try to elicit some pretext for a planned invasion. Well, they couldn't get the pretext, but they invaded anyway, killing about eighteen thousand people and continuing to occupy southern Lebanon for about twenty years with many atrocities, but all off the record because the U.S. was decisively supporting it.

Prize Atrocities

All of this peaked—the post-1982 attack, in 1985, and that was the peak year for U.S.-Israeli atrocities in southern Lebanon, what were called the Iron Fist operations; these were large-scale massacres and deportations of what the high command called "terrorist villagers." These operations, under Prime Minister Shimon Peres, are one of the candidates for the prize of the worst international terrorist crime in the peak year of 1985, remember, when terrorism was the leading story of the year.

There are other competitors. One of them, also in early 1985, was a bombing in Beirut, a car bombing. The car bombing was outside a mosque timed to go off just when everybody was leaving to insure the maximum number of casualties. It killed eighty people and wounded more than two hundred fifty, according to the *Washington Post*,[8] which gave a pretty grisly account of it. Most of them were women and girls, but it was a heavy, strong bomb, so it killed infants in their beds and all kinds of other atrocities. But that doesn't count, because it was organized by the CIA and British intelligence, so therefore it's not terrorism. So that's not really a candidate for the prize.

Now, the only possible other competitor in the peak year of 1985 was the Israeli bombing of Tunis, which killed seventy-five people; there were some grisly accounts of it in the Israeli press by good reporters. The U.S. cooperated in the atrocity by failing to inform its Tunisian ally that the bombers were on their way. George Shultz, secretary of state, immediately called the Israeli prime minister, Yitzhak Shamir, to inform him that the United States had considerable sympathy for this action, as he put it. However, Shultz drew back from open support for this international terrorism when the Security Council condemned it unanimously as an act of armed aggression, with the U.S. abstaining.

Let's continue to give Washington and its clients the benefit of the doubt, as in the case of Nicaragua,

and let's assume that the crime was only international terrorism, not the far more serious crime of
aggression, as the Security Council determined. If
it was aggression, then, observing moral truisms, we
move on to Nuremburg trials.

Those are the only three cases that come anywhere near that level in the peak year of 1985. A
couple of weeks after the Tunis bombing, Prime
Minister Peres came to Washington, where he joined
Ronald Reagan in denouncing "the evil scourge of
terrorism" in the Middle East. None of this elicited
a word of comment, and that's correct because by
convention none of it is terrorism. Recall the convention: It's only terrorism if they do it to us. When
we do much worse to them, it's not terrorism. Again,
the universal principle. Well, the Martian might
notice that, even if it's not discussable here.

I got my favorite review in history when I did write
about this some years ago. It was a review in the
Washington Post (September 18, 1988), a two-word
review by their Middle East correspondent, who
described it as "breathlessly deranged." I kind of like
that. I think he was wrong about the breathless—if
you read the article, it was pretty calm—but deranged
is correct. I mean, you have to be deranged to accept

elementary moral truisms and to describe facts that shouldn't be described. That's probably true.

Contemptible Excuses

Let's get back to the Martian. He might be puzzled about the question of why 1985 is the peak year for the return to barbarism in our time by depraved opponents of civilization itself, referring to international terrorism in the Middle East. He'd be puzzled because the worst cases by far of international terrorism in the region just are down the memory hole, like international terrorism in Central America. And lots of other cases. Current ones, in fact.

However, some cases from 1985 are remembered, well remembered, and rightly, because they are terrorism. The official prize for terrorism for that year goes to the hijacking of the *Achille Lauro* and the murder of a crippled American, Leon Klinghoffer. Everyone knows about that one. Correctly; it was a terrible atrocity. Now, of course, the perpetrators of that atrocity described it as retaliation for the Tunis bombing a week earlier, a vastly worse case of international terrorism, but quite rightly we dismissed that excuse with the contempt that it deserves.

And all of those who do not regard themselves as cowards and hypocrites will take the same principled stand with regard to all other violent acts of retaliation, including, for example, the war in Afghanistan, which remember was undertaken with the clear and unambiguous expectation that it might drive millions of people over the edge of starvation. As I said, we'll never know. For principled reasons.

Or lesser atrocities, such as those retaliations in the Israeli-occupied territories right now—with full U.S. support, as always, so they're not terrorism. The Martian would surely report on page one that the United States right now is once again using the pretext of the war on terror to protect and probably escalate terrorism by its leading client state.

The latest phase of this began on October 1, 2000. From October 1, the first days after the current Intifada began, Israeli helicopters began to attack unarmed Palestinians with missiles, killing and wounding dozens of them. There wasn't any pretext of self-defense. [Side comment: When you read the phrase "Israeli helicopters" you should understand it to mean U.S. helicopters with Israeli pilots, provided in the certain knowledge of how they are going to be used.]

Clinton immediately responded to the atrocity. On October 3, 2000, two days later, he arranged to send Israel the largest shipment of military helicopters in a decade along with spare parts for Apache attack helicopters that had been sent in mid-September. The press cooperated by refusing to report any of this—not failing, notice, but refusing; they knew all about it.

Last month the Martian press would certainly have headlined Washington's intervention to expedite the further escalation of the cycle of terror there. On December 14, the U.S. vetoed a Security Council resolution calling for implementation of the Mitchell proposals and sending international observers to monitor reduction of violence. It went at once to the General Assembly, where it was opposed by the U.S. and Israel also; therefore, it disappears. And you can check the coverage.

A week earlier, there was a conference in Geneva of the high contracting parties of the Fourth Geneva Convention, who are obliged by solemn treaty to enforce it. The Convention, as you know, was instituted after World War II to criminalize the atrocities of the Nazis. The Convention strictly bars virtually everything the U.S. and Israel do in the

NOAM CHOMSKY

occupied territories, including the settlements that were established and expanded with U.S. funding and full support, increasing under Clinton and Barak during the Camp David negotiations. Israel alone rejects this interpretation.

When the issue came to the Security Council in October 2000, the U.S. abstained, apparently not wanting to take such a blatant stand in violation of fundamental principles of international law, particularly given the circumstances of their enactment. The Security Council therefore voted fourteen-zero to call upon Israel to uphold the Convention, which it was again flagrantly violating. Pre-Clinton, the U.S. had voted with the other members to condemn Israel's "flagrant violations" of the Convention. That's consistent with the Clinton practice of effectively rescinding international law and earlier UN decisions for Israel-Palestine.

The media tell us that Arabs believe that the Convention applies to the territories, which is not false, although there's kind of an omission—the Arabs and everybody else. The December 5, 2001, meeting, including all of the European Union, reaffirmed the applicability of the Convention to the territories, the illegality of settlements; called on Israel, meaning the U.S. and Israel, to observe international law. The U.S. boycotted the meeting, thereby killing it. You can check the coverage again.

These acts again contributed to the escalation of terrorism there, including its most severe component, and the media contributed in the usual way.

Responses to Terrorism

Suppose, finally, that we join the Martian observer and we depart from convention radically. We accept moral truisms. If we can rise to that level, we can then, and only then, honestly raise the question of how to respond to terrorist crimes.

One answer is to follow the precedent of law-abiding states, the Nicaraguan precedent, for example. Of course that failed, because they ran up against the fact that the world is ruled by force, not by law, but it wouldn't fail for the U.S. However, evidently that's excluded. I have yet to see one phrase referring to that precedent in the massive coverage of the last couple of months.

Another answer was given by Bush and Boyce, but we instantly reject that one because nobody believes that Haiti or Nicaragua or Cuba and a long list of others around the world have the right to carry out massive terrorist attacks against the United States and its clients, or other rich and powerful states.

A more reasonable answer was given by a number of sources, including the Vatican, and was spelled out by the preeminent Anglo-American military historian, Michael Howard, last October. Actually, it's published in the current issue of *Foreign Affairs* (January-February 2002); that's the leading establishment journal. Now Howard has all the appropriate credentials, a lot of prestige; he's a great admirer of the British Empire, even more extravagantly of its successor in global rule, so he can't be accused of moral relativism or other such crimes.

Referring to September 11, he recommended a police operation against a criminal conspiracy whose members should be hunted down and brought before an international court, where they could receive a fair trial, and if found guilty be awarded an appropriate sentence. That was never contemplated, of course, but it sounds kind of reasonable to me. If it is reasonable, then it ought to hold for even worse terrorist crimes. For example, the U.S. international terrorist attack against Nicaragua, or even worse ones nearby and elsewhere going up to the present. That could never be contemplated, of course, but for opposite reasons.

So honesty leaves us with a dilemma. The easy answer is conventional hypocrisy. The other option is the one adopted by our Martian friend, who actually abides by the principles that we profess with grand self-righteousness. That option is harder to consider, but imperative if the world is to be spared still worse disasters.

Notes
1.   *New York Times*, 18 October1985.
2.   *Washington Post*, 26 October 1984.
3.   See essays by Jack Spence and Eldon Kenworthy in Thomas Walker, ed., *Reagan vs. the Sandinistas* (Boulder: Westview, 1987).
4.   See Noam Chomsky, *Necessary Illusions* (Boston: South End, 1989), for some comment and sources.
5.   *Liberation*, September-October 1967. Reprinted in Noam Chomsky, *American Power and the New Mandarins* (New York: Pantheon, 1969).
6.   *Envío*, March 1994.
7.   *Jerusalem Post*, 16 August 1981.
8.   *Washington Post Weekly*, 14 March 1988.

ABOUT THE AUTHOR

NOAM CHOMSKY is a world renowned political activist, writer, and professor of linguistics at Massachusetts Institute of Technology where he has taught since 1955. Chomsky has written and lectured widely on linguistics, philosophy, and politics. His most recent book is *Hegemony or Survival*. Among his other works are *Powers and Prospects*; *World Orders, Old and New*; *Deterring Democracy*; *Manufacturing Consent* (with E. S. Herman); *Year 501: The Conquest Continues*; *Profit Over People*; The *New Military Humanism*; *Rogue States*; *A New Generation Draws the Line*, and the international bestseller, *9-11*.

ABOUT SEVEN STORIES PRESS

SEVEN STORIES PRESS is an independent book publisher based in New York City, with distribution throughout the United States, Canada, England, and Australia. We publish works of the imagination by such writers as Nelson Algren, Octavia E. Butler, Assia Djebar, Ariel Dorfman, Lee Stringer, and Kurt Vonnegut, to name a few, together with political titles by voices of conscience, including the Boston Women's Health Book Collective, Project Censored, Barbara Seaman, Greg Palast, Nat Hentoff, Robert Scheer and Howard Zinn, among many others. Our books appear in hardcover, paperback, pamphlet, and e-book formats, in English and in Spanish. We believe publishers have a special responsibility to defend free speech and human rights wherever we can.

For more information about us, visit www.sevenstories.com or write for a free catalogue to Seven Stories Press, 140 Watts Street, New York, NY 10013.

ABOUT OPEN MEDIA PAMPHLETS AND BOOKS

OPEN MEDIA is a movement-oriented publishing project committed to the vision of "one world in which many worlds fit"— a world with social justice, democracy, and human rights for all people. Founded during wartime in 1991, Open Media has a ten year history of producing critically acclaimed and best-selling books and pamphlets that address the most urgent political and social issues of our time.

Before and after September 11, Open Media has produced an array of books that focus on terrorism, propaganda, public resistance, militarism, media, and the implications of U.S. foreign and domestic policies on global security and civil liberties. These titles include:

9-11 by Noam Chomsky

Acts of Aggression by Noam Chomsky with Edward W. Said

Artists in Times of War by Howard Zinn

Bin Laden, Islam, and America's New "War on Terrorism" by As`ad AbuKhalil

Colombia and the United States: War, Unrest and Destabilization by Mario Murillo

Full Spectrum Dominance: U.S. Power in Iraq and Beyond by Rahul Mahajan

Global Governance: The Battle for Planetary Power by Kristin Dawkins

Information War: American Propaganda, Free Speech, and Opinion Control Since 9-11 by Nancy Snow

**AVAILABLE OCTOBER 2002 FROM
THE OPEN MEDIA SERIES**

OUR MEDIA, NOT THEIRS
The Democratic Struggle Against Corporate Media

by Robert W. McChesney & John Nichols
Foreword by Noam Chomsky

"An astute analysis offering compassionate solutions.
I loved the book. It speaks for me."

—PATTI SMITH

"McChesney and Nichols both critically assess our
current media system and, even better, help us
to imagine something different, mapping the
transition from a period of individual frustration
with corporate media toward one of collective
action for their reform."

—JANINE JACKSON

ISBN: 1-58322-549-8 | $9.95 | www.sevenstories.com